NEW CAREER OPTIONS: A WOMAN'S GUIDE

Women's Studies Series

Women A Bibliography on Their Education and Careers
Astin, H. S., Ph.D., Suniewick, N., Dweck, S., M.A.

Women in the Work Force
Katzell, Mildred E., Ph.D., Byham, W. C., Ph.D.

New Career Options for Women: A Selected Annotated Bibliography
Phelps, A. T., Ed.D., Farmer, H. S., Ph.D., Backer, T. E., Ph.D.

New Career Options: A Woman's Guide
Farmer, H. S., Ph.D., Backer, T. E., Ph.D.

New Career Options for Women: A Counselor's Sourcebook
Farmer, H. S., Ph.D., Backer, T. E., Ph.D.

New Career Options: A Woman's Guide

Helen S. Farmer, Ph.D.
Thomas E. Backer, Ph.D.

Human Interaction Research Institute
10889 Wilshire Boulevard
Los Angeles, California
October 1976

Prepared under funding support by
the National Institute of Education
Contract No. NIE-C-74-0100

HUMAN SCIENCES PRESS
Formerly BEHAVIORAL PUBLICATIONS INC.
72 FIFTH AVENUE, NEW YORK, N.Y. 10011

Library of Congress Catalog Number 77-853

ISBN: 0-87705-272-7

Copyright © 1977 by Human Sciences Press
72 Fifth Avenue, New York, New York 10011

Printed in the United States of America
789 987654321

Library of Congress Cataloging in Publication Data

Farmer, Helen S
  New career options.

  "National Institute of Education contract no. NIE-C-74-0100."
  1. Vocational guidance for women—United States.
2. Women—Employment—United States. I. Backer,
Thomas E., joint author. II. Title.
HD6058.F37   331.7'02'024042   77-853

Contents

6

As you read this, you may be waiting to see a career counselor because you want to make some decisions about your place in the world of work. You may be young, and thinking about college or some kind of training program. Or you may be a working woman now, and wondering about how to make a change in the work you're doing. Or you may be a homemaker with grown children, wanting to get back to work.

If you're not seeing a counselor right now, you may want to find out what you can do on your own.

There's never been a better time for women and girls to think hard about what they want to do for a living, about what careers look good to them, and about how to improve their work situation.

Things *are* looking up: Women are becoming leaders of nations all over the world. In our own country, more and more women are gaining political power. Women also are getting more and better jobs as executives in major companies like IBM or General Motors. And women are successfully doing jobs their mothers or grandmothers wouldn't have dreamed of—repairing telephone lines, driving buses, operating heavy machinery.

New laws help make sure that women get treated fairly on the job, and in school or training.

Women's liberation is part of our time.

Still, there are many problems a girl or woman has to watch out for when looking for a job, for schooling or training. Discrimination still happens: women sometimes don't get the job they want and are qualified for, just because they are female. Too often, women don't get promoted when they deserve to. Other women are afraid to go after a job because "it isn't feminine" or "my husband wouldn't like it." Still others don't even know for sure where the good chances for work and training really are!

WHAT THIS BOOKLET IS ABOUT

On the pages that follow, we talk about what work is like for women in the 1970's, about what the problems are and how to overcome them. The booklet tells about attitudes women sometimes have about themselves (or beliefs their husbands or bosses hold) that get in the way of finding good work opportunities. Some new laws related to work for women are described. And we talk *solutions*— how to get help in planning a career or schooling; how to get a job.

If you're seeing a counselor now, what's in here may add to the things you talk to your counselor about, to the questions you may want to ask. Making a good career choice often is easier with a trained professional to help you. If you *don't* have a counselor to go to right now, the last section of the booklet may help you, since it gives lists of reading materials, and places you can go to or write to for more information.

How The Booklet Is Set Up

The rest of this pamphlet deals with the following questions:

- What are the new opportunities for American women at work?
- What problems still remain?
- What are the chances for women who want to work in the crafts?
- What are the chances for women in management?
- What are the chances for women in the professions?
- What are the new laws, and what do they mean?
- How can a woman combine marriage, family and a career?
- How can a woman return to work after being a housewife and mother?
- What mistaken beliefs are standing in your way?
- How can a woman or girl get help in planning for a career?
- How can education or training opportunities be found?
- How should a girl or woman look for a job?
- How can a person get more information?

When you've read the discussion of these questions, maybe you'll want to ask yourself at least two more questions:

How can I use what I've learned here?
What information or help do I still need?

A counselor can help in answering both these questions, or you can turn to the last section here to start searching out some of your own answers.

What Are The New Opportunities For American Women At Work?

MORE WOMEN ARE WORKING THAN EVER BEFORE: Many more women work in the 1970's as opposed to the 1960's. Nine out of ten girls today will work at some time in their lives. More than 50% of all women ages 18 to 64 are holding down jobs right now.

MORE MOTHERS ARE WORKING: Four out of ten now, as opposed to only four out of a *hundred* mothers with children under 18 back in 1940. Even for mothers with preschool-age children, three out of ten are working today.

This means, of course, that the old pattern of "interrupted" careers for women who stopped working to raise families is changing.

EDUCATION HELPS: Women who have college degrees are more likely to be working today than women with less than four years of college. Women with graduate degrees are even more likely to work than those with only bachelor's degrees.

MORE OPPORTUNITIES FOR MINORITY WOMEN: Minority women have made gains over the last ten years in the world of work. They are earning more, and education and salary gaps between white and minority women are closing. (Still, far more black teenagers than white are unemployed.)

What Problems Still Remain?

Despite all these good changes, the fact that this booklet is needed suggests that discrimination is still a very real problem for working women in America. Much too often, these women still
•get paid less than men for equal work
•don't advance as far as their abilities would permit them to
•can't get certain kinds of jobs at all.

Women who work full-time, on the average, get paid only 60% as much as men who have similar jobs. In fact, the gap in earnings between men and women hasn't really changed much in the last 20 years! (Women are more likely to get equal pay if they work in professional or technical jobs.)

Certain kinds of jobs are still thought of as most suitable for women, while others are saved only for men—even though this is now illegal. The following chart shows the differences for several occupational groups.

So, the picture isn't all good! We are taking an optimistic point of view in this booklet, and there certainly are many new opportunities for women to get better jobs, new kinds of jobs. Women who try to do this, though, should be aware that they will have many prejudices and other obstacles to work against. More about these later.

WHAT ARE THE CHANCES FOR WOMEN WHO WANT TO WORK IN THE CRAFTS?

Many more women have been getting jobs in the crafts since 1970. Before 1960, only 2 or 3 per cent of all craft workers were women. By 1974, though, about 5 out of every 100 craft workers were female.

Many women are now working as bakers, bookbinders, decorators, furriers, opticians, lens grinders, and tailors.

Aircraft mechanic, auto mechanic, carpenter, electrician, machinist, and telephone installer or repairer are other crafts where women now are starting to get some of the available jobs.

It used to be that employers said women as a group don't have the natural skill, or the physical strength, to do most of these jobs. Experience has shown that just isn't true.

Until recently, many women stayed away from the crafts because they visualized a repairman in dirty overalls, a construction worker risking life and limb on a high scaffold, or an auto mechanic under the body of a car. These mental pictures weren't very attractive to most American women.

But women today are realizing that a person employed in a skilled trade may be more independent, can be outdoors more of the time, and can earn more than those who hold traditional "women's jobs" like secretary.

WHAT ARE THE CHANCES FOR WOMEN IN MANAGEMENT?

Almost one-fifth of all business executives today are women. Women also are doing well in the management branch of govern-

11

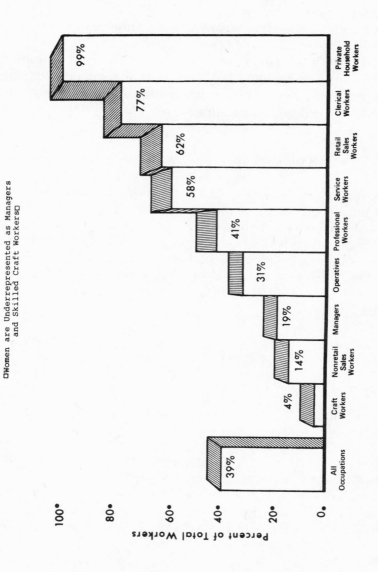

☐Women are Underrepresented as Managers and Skilled Craft Workers☐

Percent of Total Workers

All Occupations — 39%
Craft Workers — 4%
Nonretail Sales Workers — 14%
Managers — 19%
Operatives — 31%
Professional Workers — 41%
Service Workers — 58%
Retail Sales Workers — 62%
Clerical Workers — 77%
Private Household Workers — 99%

Source: Prepared by the Women's Bureau, Employment Standards Administration, from April 1973 data published by the Bureau of Labor Statistics, U.S. Department of Labor.

ment—politics. For example, in 1974 eighteen women were elected to the U.S. House of Representatives, a record for any one election. Women became governors (Connecticut), mayors (San Jose, California), chief justices and lieutenant governors (New York), and secretaries of state (California).

In the 1970's, many new positions are expected to open up for women in management. Partly because of some new federal laws, companies are eager to get women into their management trainee programs, and even into upper-level jobs.

What Are The Chances For Women In The Professions?

Women's participation in the professions has always been high, but until recently it was mostly in fields like nursing, elementary school teaching, and library science. New laws now make it easier for women to get into training programs for the professions, and with continuing shortages of new workers in many fields, new opportunities are coming along every day.

All of these professions will offer more opportunities for women in the 1970's:

- Accountant
- Architect
- Chemist
- Dentist
- Dietician
- Economist
- Electrical engineer
- Mathematician
- Medical records librarian
- Physician
- Physicist
- Psychologist
- Public relations worker
- Rehabilitation counselor
- School counselor
- Social worker
- Speech pathologist
- Veterinarian

For almost all these, of course, some subfields will be better than others. For example, in elementary school teaching, specialists in individual instruction or special education for the retarded are more in demand right now than regular teachers. Legal records librarians and information specialists for private industry are especially promising library science fields.

In the nursing field, employment opportunities are expected to remain good through 1985 for registered nurses, nursing aides and licensed practical nurses. Particularly good chances are expected in related health occupations, such as physical therapist and medical technician.

What Are The New Laws, And What Do They Mean?

A number of laws have been passed in the last few years that can help protect women all over the United States from discrimination in employment or in schooling and training, and that offer them other benefits as well.

TWO LAWS ABOUT DISCRIMINATION IN EDUCATION AND TRAINING: A law called "Title IX of the Education Amendments of 1972" says that no college, university or vocational school can discriminate against women if it gets any federal support money. "Title VII and Title VIII of the Public Health Service Act" say basically the same thing, but apply specifically to training programs for health care workers like doctors and nurses. These two laws have helped open up many opportunities for women to get into training that will lead to the career they want.

TWO LAWS ABOUT EMPLOYMENT: "Executive Order 11246" says that any organization which has a contract with the federal government for more than $10,000 cannot discriminate on the basis of sex when hiring employees. Discrimination in salaries, job upgrading and training also is illegal. "Title VII of the Civil Rights Act of 1964" is even more general: it makes sex discrimination illegal in any place of business with more than 15 employees. This is the law on which all the work of the Equal Employment Opportunity Commission is based.

Equal Pay Act

This act makes illegal discrimination in *pay* for similar work. This law is working, too: for 1973 alone, payments of some $18 million in back pay were made to 30,000 American women workers, and for only the first six months of 1974—$36 million (some from court judgments, others out of court)!

Protective Legislation

The Equal Employment Opportunity Commission has ruled that laws preventing women from working overtime, and other so-called "protective legislation," are illegal. By the end of 1973, 39 of the 40 states that used to have protective legislation defining maximum daily or weekly work hours repealed those laws, or modified their enforcement in the light of that ruling.

Maternity Leave

The Civil Rights Act also made maternity leave with full reemployment rights more available to women workers. In 1974, 3 out of 4 women who needed it received such leave. Childbirth, miscarriage, and abortion now have to be covered by company health insurance plans and sick leave policies.

Child Care Tax Benefits

You may deduct child care expenses from your income tax if your income does not exceed $27,600. If you are married and your joint income is over $18,000, your deduction is reduced 50¢ for each dollar of additional income. For the majority of working mothers, this means that child care expenses of up to $400 a month can be deducted.

In the Future: Equal Rights Amendment

By early 1974, 33 states had passed the Equal Rights Amendment (38 are required for ratification). This amendment says that all state and local governments, and the federal government, must always treat men and women equally. This amendment, incidentally, was first introduced in 1923!

HOW CAN A WOMAN COMBINE MARRIAGE, FAMILY, AND A CAREER?

Many working women feel guilty about neglecting their children or home. Having to handle all these responsibilities at once can be quite a hassle. Changing some attitudes and beliefs about working mothers can help reduce guilt. Feeling less hassled and overworked calls for better planning and use of one's time.

Efforts to decrease the burden imposed on working women by their combined roles as worker-homemaker-mother are being made in a number of ways:

1. New kinds of household service workers are available who put housecleaning services more within the financial reach of women who couldn't afford full-time servants. Whole teams of workers clean a house in an hour or two; these services are patterned after business office cleanup crews.

2. Dry cleaners, post offices, grocery and other stores are beginning to stay open evenings and Sundays so that the working wife can manage her responsibilities more easily.

3. Doctors, dentists, and other professionals also are beginning to offer hours more convenient for the working mother.

4. More child care options are open. Many child care facilities sponsored by the government have opened up, for example, to welfare mothers on the WIN program. Some business organizations (Polaroid and the Ford Foundation are two examples) provide a child care allowance to employees with small children, leaving mothers free to select their own child care facility. Some unions—e.g., the United Federation of Teachers in New York City—have set up child care centers.

5. Part-time work with flexible hours is becoming more common. More than a third of all women who work have part-time jobs right now. Some part-time employment is traditional, like private household services or farm labor. However, some new part-time arrangements are being developed in health care, teaching and other fields, particularly where shortages of workers exist:

   Paired: Two people share one full-time job. Each has equal responsibility for the job, and they may cover for each other if one is ill. Teachers, doctors, lawyers, and radio or television news announcers are some occupations for which this kind of arrangement has been tried.

   Shared: Two persons divide a job between them; each is responsible for *half* the work. This is good for social workers, customer relations people, or other jobs that have activities can be divided up easily (by clients, cases, etc.).

   Split-level: Some tasks that are part of a single "full-time job" can be given to one person, the rest to somebody else. This is well-suited for administrative jobs which also require clerical and secretarial skills. By dividing the work between two people at different "levels" of skill, an employer can have two employees doing one job at salary levels right for the kind of work actually done.

Specialist: A specialist can be employed part-time to do a given task. Examples are consultants in various fields, personnel interviewers, foreign language teachers, or editors of corporation newsletters.

How Can A Woman Return To Work After Being A Housewife And Mother?

Being older, having had children, or being divorced need not constitute handicaps to getting a good job. Discrimination in hiring based on age is illegal—the "Age Discrimination in Employment Act" prohibits it. Sometimes experience in handling a household, or arranging schooling of your children, can be valuable assets to an employer. For the divorced woman, special counseling facilities have been developed in many community centers, churches, and college settings.

Some women may need to get training before trying to get back to work. There are several ways to do this. One is through continuing education programs where more than half a million women are enrolled today at colleges, universities, and vocational schools across the country. Some women may want to obtain academic credit for experience or knowledge they already have through the General Educational Development (GED) tests for a high school certificate, or the College Level Examination Program (CLEP) for college credit. Also, volunteer work for a charity or museum can sometimes be a way to get started, although unpaid work like this is rarely a good long-term goal.

What Mistaken Beliefs Are Standing In Your Way?

Many attitudes girls or women have—and their employers, parents, or husbands, too—do hinder developing their full potential in the world of work. The barriers these attitudes create can be just as damaging as actual discrimination. Very often, though, such attitudes change when confronted by the facts. For example:

Belief
Women don't want responsibility on the job; they don't want promotions or job changes which add to their work load.

Fact

Relatively few women have been offered positions of real responsibility. But when given these opportunities, women, like men, do cope with job responsibilities in addition to personal or family responsibilities. In 1973, 4.7 million women held professional and technical jobs, another 1.6 million worked as nonfarm managers and administrators. Many others held supervisory jobs at all levels in offices and factories.

Belief

Women aren't serious about working—they work only for extra pocket money.

Fact

Nearly half of all women work because they need the money! They are single, widowed, divorced, or separated or have husbands whose incomes are very low.

Belief

Women are out ill more than male workers; they cost the company more.

Fact

A recent government study showed no real differences in absenteeism rates due to illness or injury.

Belief

Women don't work as long or as regularly as their male coworkers.

Fact

Fewer women today leave work for marriage and having children. But even for those who do, the majority return when their children are in school. Even with a break in employment, the average woman worker will be employed 25 years, as compared with 43 years for the average male workers. The single woman averages 45 years at work.

Belief

Married women take jobs away from men.

Fact

There were almost 20 million married women (with husbands living at home) in the labor force in March 1973; the number of unemployed men was 2.5 million. If all the married women stayed home and unemployed men were put in their jobs, there would be 17.3 million unfilled jobs!

Belief

Women should stick to "women's jobs" and shouldn't compete for "men's jobs."

Fact

Jobs, with extremely rare exceptions, are sexless. Tradition rather than job content has led to labeling certain jobs as women's and others as men's.

Belief

A woman's place is in the home.

Fact

Homemaking in itself is no longer a full-time job for most people. Goods and services formerly produced in the home are now commercially available; labor-saving devices lighten or eliminate much work around the house.

Belief

Women should have primary responsibility for raising children.

Fact

Studies do indicate that women all over the world are expected to assume primary responsibility for child rearing. However, attitudes of many husbands *are* changing, from expecting that wives will do most or all of the child-rearing tasks, to the view that child rearing tasks are to be shared. The trend to smaller families will make child rearing tasks less time-consuming than before. A woman who wants to work can choose a husband, if she wishes, who will share responsibility when the children are sick, need help with their homework, or are in trouble with the law.

Belief

A college education is wasted on girls.

Fact

The fact is the more education a girl has the more likely she is to work. Nine out of ten women with PhD degrees were still working

8 years after earning their degree. Sixty-eight percent of women with university degrees continue to work, whereas only 28% of women with an elementary school education work, and half of women who graduate from high school continue working.

Belief

Girls are not interested in "scientific things."

Fact

Researchers have found that girls perform as well as boys in math and science up to about age 10; thereafter, their performance becomes increasingly poorer. This effect may be due, at least in part, to parents and teachers praising boys for scientific interests and not praising girls. Encouraging girls to take available math and science courses is one way to modify girls' attitudes. Also, rewarding girls for achievements in math and science could help.

Similarly, encouraging girls to take shop and technical subjects such as drafting could help change girls' attitudes about their mechanical abilities and "spatial relations" aptitudes. Some states require shop and home economics for both girls and boys in elementary school.

Belief

If a woman succeeds in a career, she will be less feminine and men will reject her.

Fact

Having a career does not necessarily lead to failure in marriage or love. Many highly trained women are married and a majority of these reported that they found their husbands supportive and encouraging of their career.

Belief

Women are naturally passive and dependent, while men are active, independent, initiating, and dominant.

Fact

The role of woman and mother is not biologically more passive and dependent than that of man and father. Research indicates that dominance related to persuasion, task competence, and ability to lead others is found equally in men and in women.

How Can A Woman Or Girl Get Help In Planning For A Career?

In order to make a good career choice you should have information about yourself—your interests, values, abilities, and skills—as well as information about work opportunities and the training required to get into various jobs. It's particularly important to have good information about what the problems and barriers are in getting into a particular kind of work, so that you can plan *early* to overcome these obstacles.

If you are in a school setting, or can go to one for career planning help, your most useful resource will probably be a *counselor*.

Many high schools today have career planning centers, some of them funded by the federal government as part of career education programs.

In a college or university, you also may enroll in a *course* which offers career counseling, both in the classroom and in individual sessions with a counselor. Such courses provide guidance in self-assessment, preparing to look for a job, writing a resume, learning how to give a good interview, and so forth. If you get into a course where you work closely with other girls and women who are making career decisions, you can get lots of moral support—and give some—that will help, too.

Even if you are not a student, you can often enroll in a counseling class like this through an extension or continuing education program. Community colleges as well as universities often offer such courses. For the woman returning to work after being a housewife, the psychological support such a course provides may be essential. These courses are often called "bridging groups" because they give both skills and the *confidence* necessary to move from the home back into the office, or back into school for further training.

Individual counseling, of course, is usually available for students in colleges and universities. This can be helpful in addition to courses in career planning, particularly if you face unusual obstacles in getting to your chosen career goal, or if you are very uncertain about what kind of work you'd like to get into.

Some college and university career planning services offer counseling to non-students as well, though usually for a much higher fee. As opposed to an extension class on career planning, this can give you more individualized attention and can be scheduled to suit you.

Some government agencies, such as employment services and manpower training programs, offer a limited amount of career planning help. If you go to such an agency, you should keep in mind that they are in business mostly to get you a job or into a training program, rather than for general career development.

The YWCA in several cities offers special career counseling services to women, as do B'nai Brith and Professional Women's Clubs. The quality of these services is high, and they should be considered if an office is conveniently located for you.

There also are many private sources for career planning, from individual counselors and counseling agencies, through services offered by professional societies for women who plan to enter a particular profession.

To a certain extent, you can even do your own counseling just by keeping up on current job and training opportunities. Regular reading of publications containing such information is the best way to do this (see last section of this booklet for examples).

How Can Education Or Training Opportunities Be Found?

Many women's studies courses and programs have been started in the last four years on campuses across the nation. At last count, at least 32 campuses offer a major in women's studies. More than 800 courses for women are listed in recent college catalogs. Such courses can be valuable additions to other classes a girl or woman may take, because they can do a lot to build confidence and encourage self-exploration.

There also are numerous opportunities for women today to get subsidized, even free, training for work in the crafts. Preapprenticeship programs in high schools and community colleges are beginning to admit women in fields like air conditioning repair, auto body and fender repair, carpentry, and metalworking. More women also are getting into training programs at community manpower agencies, and into on-the-job training programs in private industry.

Continuing education programs for women who want to come back to work after being a housewife are widely available. These programs can include many extra services, such as child care, financial aid, and flexible scheduling of coursework. General orientation courses also are available, which provide guest lectures on careers by women who've been successful in various fields, information about training opportunities, counseling and help in getting a job.

Courses that train women to work in certain fields may be offered in schools or manpower programs. Teacher aides, library aides, mental health assistants, nursery school aides, research assistants, and so forth are among the job categories for which women can receive training.

HOW SHOULD A GIRL OR WOMAN LOOK FOR A JOB?

Training in how to look for the right job is offered in many continuing education programs for women. Career planning centers often provide education in this area, sometimes including practice job interviews with videotape to give feedback.

Naturally, a counselor may be of help in planning for a job search. The individual woman or girl can do much to help herself as well. Using a "personal resource network" of friends and family to identify likely jobs can be particularly useful—a little "influence" of this sort can make all the difference in getting a job.

Most sizable American towns have Employment Service offices where a girl or woman can get direct help in finding a job—there are even listings you can use yourself to get job interviews. In some states, these public agencies are called by other names, but you can find out by calling city hall or a similar office. Private employment agencies can help you with job-hunting, too, though you should be very careful to learn who pays for their services before you let them help you (most good agencies charge the company that hires you, *not you*).

Often people start job hunting by looking at the want ads in the newspaper. Reputable firms usually have ads for several openings, and they tell you specifically what the job involves. If the ad seems vague to you, call and find out more about it before going in for an interview. Very large employers—a big factory, a university—also may have job listings on display in their employment offices.

For almost any job involving skills or training—from secretary to corporation president—you need to have a *resume*. Get help from a counselor or career course, if you can, in writing up a resume. This piece of paper is often the first chance a possible employer has to evaluate you, so it's important! There are many styles in resumes, but almost all include these things:

EDUCATION AND TRAINING

Where you've gone to school, and when
What degrees you have (high school
diploma, A.A., B.A., etc.)
What special training you have

WORK EXPERIENCE

All full-time or part-time jobs you've
had including dates of employment

PERSONAL DATA

Age
Home address and telephone number
Marital status

REFERENCES

Either work-related (a supervisor) or personal
(e.g., your minister)

An attractive, informative one or two page resume can help a lot in getting you into the right job.

HOW CAN A PERSON GET MORE INFORMATION?

All of the questions mentioned above may be very important to girls or women who have career decisions to make. No doubt some of these have been very much on your mind, and you didn't need this booklet to raise the question! The answers we've given here are designed to raise *other questions* for you, though—questions about choices you have in getting the school, training, or job opportunity you want.

If you are seeing a counselor right now, the best place to bring up these new questions is in your next counseling session. For example, if you want some specific skills in preparing a resume and how to do interviews, ask your counselor where you might be able to take a course that would help.

The remaining pages of this booklet can be used by girls and women who, at least right now, don't have a regular counselor to turn to. The books and other resources we list here can help you learn some skills and make some decisions for yourself—or get you in touch with a counselor, career development center, or education program. These suggestions are organized in approximately the same order as the booklet itself.

ABOUT WOMEN IN MANAGEMENT

Two books to read are R. Loring & T. Wells' *Breakthrough into Management* (New York: Van Nostrand Reinhold, 1972), and H. Kahne's *Women in Management: Strategy for Increase* (Washington, D.C.: Business and Professional Women's Foundation, 1974).

ABOUT DISCRIMINATION IN EMPLOYMENT

For 64¢, you can get a helpful booklet from the U.S. Department of Labor Women's Bureau (Washington, D.C.), called *A Working Woman's Guide to Her Job Rights.* Free of charge from the Office for Civil Rights, Department of Health Education & Welfare in Washington is *Sex Discrimination,* also a booklet.

EQUAL RIGHTS AMENDMENT

If you want to know more about this Constitutional Amendment, one source is an article in the *Women Lawyer's Journal,* Winter 1973, volume 59, pp. 11–14, by E. L. Chittick, who is the National Chairperson of the organization that initiated this Amendment more than 40 years ago. Another resource is a booklet, *Interpretation of the Equal Rights Amendment in Accordance with Legislative History,* published in 1974 and available from the Citizen's Advisory Council on the Status of Women, Room 1336, Department of Labor Building, Washington, D.C. 20210.

WORKING MOTHERS

An entertaining book that also offers many practical tips for the working mother is Alice Skelsey's *The Working Mother's Guide to Her Home, Her Family and Herself* (New York: Random House, 1970).

CHILD CARE

A useful booklet, *Day Care Facts* (Pamphlet 16, 1973) is available from the U.S. Department of Labor, Women's Bureau, Washington, D.C., 20210. Industrial day care centers (where child care is available for a fee) are listed in Bulletin 296 from the same place.

GENERAL EDUCATIONAL DEVELOPMENT (GED) TESTS AND COLLEGE LEVEL EXAMINATION PROGRAM (CLEP) TESTS

The U.S. Department of Labor, Women's Bureau has prepared a brochure, *Get Credit for What You Know* (Leaflet 56, 1974) that outlines how to take these exams.

FOR DIVORCEES

Back in Circulation by Jean Block (New York: Macmillan, 1969) and *The Divorced Mother: A Guide to Readjustment* by Carol Mindy (New York: McGraw-Hill, 1970) are helpful resources. The second book gives some specific information on legal aspects of divorce.

CAREER PLANNING

CATALYST Publications offers a *Self-Guidance Series* including *Planning for Work* and *Your Job Campaign,* available from CATALYST (6 E. 82nd Street, New York, N.Y. 10028) at $1.25 each. CATALYST's list of resource centers for women is reproduced at the end of this booklet.

The American Personnel and Guidance Association publishes a directory of accredited counseling agencies, available for $3.00

from the Association at 1607 New Hampshire Avenue, N.W., Washington, D.C. 20009 (or a copy may be available in your local library).

Sixty-seven organizations having units devoted to career-related services for women are given at the end of this booklet.

For self-exploration, one valuable resource is *Planning Ahead After Forty,* by Milton E. Hahn (Los Angeles: Western Psychological Services, 1967). This book was developed for adult women and men, and provides a set of self-assessment exercises which could be used by women independently, in groups, or with a counselor.

Joyce Mitchell's *Other Choices for Becoming a Woman* (Pittsburgh: Know, Inc., 1974) is a publication high school girls might find helpful in making career choices.

Knowing The Job Market

The Women's Bureau, U.S. Department of Labor, has regularly updated publications that can be useful to women in keeping informed about job opportunities. They have publications on women in the skilled trades, careers for women in the 70's, and a series, "Why Not Be—an Apprentice? (Engineer? Medical Technologist? Technical Writer? Urban Planner? Optometrist?)". Most of these publications are available free, or for a small fee, from the Women's Bureau. (See last section of this booklet for address). CATALYST publications has an education opportunities series, and a career opportunities series outlining career *paths* in 27 fields, many of them nontraditional.

Students at Stanford University also have prepared special publications for women in law, engineering, and medicine. These publications are available by writing to the appropriate department of the University in Stanford, California.

Continuing Education

The U.S. Department of Labor, Women's Bureau has produced a helpful catalog, *Continuing Education Programs and Services for Women,* Pamphlet 10 (1971).

JOB SEARCH

Some relevant materials are: R. N. Bolles' *What Color is Your Para-chute? A Practical Manual for Job Hunters and Career Changers* (Berke-ley, Calif: Ten Speed Press, 1972); Performance Dynamics, Inc.'s *The Professional Job Hunting System: World's Fastest Way to Get a Job* (Verona, New Jersey, 1970); and Caroline Bird's *Everything A Woman Needs to Know to Get Paid What She's Worth* (New York: McKay, 1974).

In this last section, we list some sources of information on women and their careers, including periodicals, organizations which pro-duce timely material, and publishing houses.

NEWSLETTERS

The Spokeswoman

> Editor-Publisher: Susan Davis
> 5464 South Shore Drive
> Chicago, Illinois 60615
> (312) 667–3745
> Rates: $7.00 per year for individuals (monthly)
> $12.00 per year for organizations

Women Today

> Editor: Barbara Jordan Moore
> Publisher: Myra E. Barrar
> Today Publications & News Service
> National Press Building
> Washington, D.C. 20004
> (202) 628–6663
> U.S. Rates: $18.00 per year; $30.00 two years
> (*Women Today* is the only national biweekly news source de-voted exclusively to the activities of the women's movement from an unbiased and unsponsored point of view.)
> Subscribers to *Women Today* also receive free a regular report

of the Washington Chapter of the Women's Equity Action League (WEAL) which lists the progress of bills before Congress and recent court decisions affecting women.

NOW Acts (national newsletter)

NOW National Headquarters
1952 East 73rd Street, Room 106
Chicago, Illinois 60649
(312) 324–3067
Rates: $3.00 per year for non-members

Women's Rights Law Reporter

180 University Avenue
Newark, New Jersey 07102
Published quarterly

The Executive Woman

Editor: Shelley Gross
Publisher: Sandra Brown
747 Third Avenue
New York, New York 10017
Rates: $20.00 per year (10 issues)
A monthly newsletter for women in business.

On Campus with Women

Project on the Status of and Education of
Women, Association of American Colleges, 1818 R Street,
Washington, D.C. 20009.

GOVERNMENT ORGANIZATIONS PROVIDING PUBLICATIONS ABOUT WOMEN

Citizens' Advisory Council on the Status of Women
    Washington, D.C. 20210
    Director: Jacqueline G. Gutwillig

Women's Bureau, U.S. Department of Labor
    Washington, D.C. 20210
    Director: Carmen Maymi

Advisory Council on Women's Educational Programs
    Department of Health, Education & Welfare
    Contact: Women's Program Staff
        U.S. Office of Education
        Washington, D.C. 20201

NON-GOVERNMENT ORGANIZATIONS PROVIDING PUBLICATIONS ABOUT WOMEN

Project on the Status and Education of Women
    Association of American Colleges
    Director: Bernice Sandler
    1818 R Street, N.W.
    Washington, D.C. 20009

Education Commission of the States, Project to Promote Equal
    Rights for Women in Education
    300 Lincoln Tower, 1800 Lincoln Street, Denver, Colorado
    80203
    Director: Wendell Pierce

Business & Professional Women's Foundation
    2012 Massachusetts Avenue, N.W.
    Washington, D.C. 20036

National Organization for Women
    P.O. Box 114, Cathedral Station,
    New York, N.Y. 10025

Resource Center on Sex Roles in Education of the National
    Education Association
    1156 15th Street, N.W., Suite 918
    Washington, D.C. 20036

30

PUBLISHING HOUSES WITH MATERIALS AVAILABLE ON WOMEN

Association of American Colleges, 1818 "R" Street, N.W., Washington, D.C. 20009. Project on the Status and Education of Women—Bernice Sandler. Many fine publications, statistics, bibliographies, etc. Write for information.

ERIC Research Currents, The Emergence of Women's Courses in Higher Education. Publications Department, American Association for Higher Education,
One Du Pont Circle, Suite 780,
Washington, D.C. 20036. Price: $.15.

KNOW, Inc., P.O. Box 10197, Pittsburgh, Pennsylvania 15232. Send for lists—lots of good stuff! (Write same organization at P.O. Box 86031, Pittsburgh, Pennsylvania 15221 for Catalog of Feminist Children's Books.)

Nonsexist Curricular Materials for Elementary Schools, Ed. by Laurie Olsen Johnson. Order from The Clearing House on Women's Studies, The Feminist Press, Box 334, Old Westbury, New York 11568.

The Clearing House on Women's Studies, The Feminist Press, Box 334, Old Westbury, New York 11568. Excellent source for curricular materials.

CATALYST

A variety of publications are available; order from 6 East 82nd Street, New York, New York 10028, for approximately $1.00 each.

CATALYST NATIONAL NETWORK OF LOCAL RESOURCE CENTERS

CALIFORNIA

ADVOCATES FOR WOMEN, INC.
564 Market Street #218
San Francisco, Calif. 94104
(415) 989–5449

Monday–Friday, 9:00 a.m. to 5:00 p.m.
Independent non-profit agency.
Career counseling, job referral, placement.
No fees.

CALIFORNIA STATE
  UNIVERSITY, LONG BEACH
Community Counseling Center
6101 East Seventh Street, 203 Adm.
  Annex.
Long Beach, Calif. 90840
(213) 498–4001
Monday–Thursday, 8:00 a.m. to 7:00
  p.m.
Friday: 8:00 a.m. to 5:00 p.m.
Educational and career counseling,
  continuing education courses.
Registration fee. Other fees vary.

THE CLAREMONT COLLEGES
Special Academic Programs and
Office for Continuing Education
Harper Hall 160
Claremont, Calif. 91711
(714) 626–8511
Monday–Friday, 9:00 a.m. to 5:00
  p.m.
College-sponsored office.
Educational and career counseling,
  job referral, continuing education
  courses.
Registration fee.

CYPRESS COLLEGE
Career Planning Center
9200 Valley View Street
Cypress, Calif. 90630
(714) 826–2220 Ext. 221
Monday–Friday, 8:00 a.m. to 4:00
  p.m.
Monday–Thursday, 6:00 p.m. to 9:00
  p.m.
Official college office.
Educational and career counseling.
No fees.

FOOTHILL COLLEGE
Continuing Education for Women
12345 El Monte
Los Altos Hills, Calif. 94002
(415) 948–8590 Ext. 258
Monday–Friday, 10:00 a.m. to 3:00
  p.m.
Official college office.

Educational and career counseling,
  job referral, continuing education
  courses.
No fees.

MARKET PLACE, A
  MANAGEMENT
  SEARCH AGENCY
1901 Avenue of the Stars
Los Angeles, Calif. 90067
(213) 553–4088
Monday–Saturday, by appointment.
Independent private agency.
Job placement.
Fees vary.

NEW WAYS TO WORK
457 Kingsley Avenue
Palo Alto, Calif. 94301
(415) 321—WORK
Monday–Friday, 9:30 a.m. to 2:30
  p.m.
Independent non-profit agency.
Career counseling, job referral,
  placement.
No fees.

PROGRAM ADVISORY SERVICE,
  UCLA EXTENSION
10995 Le Conte Avenue, Room 215
Los Angeles, Calif. 90024
(213) 825–2401 Ext. 250 or 261
Monday–Friday, 9:00 a.m. to 5:00
  p.m.
Monday evening, 6:00 p.m. to 9:00
  p.m.
College-sponsored office.
Educational and career counseling,
  job referral information,
  continuing education courses.
No fees.

RESOURCE CENTER FOR
  WOMEN
499 Hamilton Ave. Suite 204
Palo Alto, Calif. 94301
(415) 324–1710
Monday–Thursday, 10:00 a.m. to
  3:00 p.m.

Independent non-profit agency.
Educational and career counseling,
adult education courses, job
referral, placement.
Fees vary.

UCSD EXTENSION COUNSELING
SERVICES
University of California, San Diego
P.O. Box 109
La Jolla, Calif. 92037
(714) 453-2000
Monday–Friday, 8:00 a.m. to 9:00
p.m.
Official college office.
Educational and career counseling,
continuing education courses, job
referral.
No registration fee. Other fees vary.

THE WOMEN'S OPPORTUNITIES
CENTER
Univ. of California Extension, Irvine
Irvine, Calif. 92664
(714) 833-7128
Monday–Friday, 10:00 a.m. to 4:00
p.m.
College sponsored office.
Educational and career counseling,
continuing education courses.
No fees.

WOMEN'S PLACE, INC.
1901 Avenue of the Stars
Los Angeles, Calif. 90067
(213) 553-0870
Monday–Friday, 9:30 a.m. to 2:30
p.m.
Independent private.
Career counseling, workshops, job
referral, 5-hour day.
Fees vary.

COLORADO

COLORADO STATE UNIVERSITY
Women's Programs
Center for Continuing Education

Ft. Collins, Colorado 80521
(303) 491-5288
Monday–Friday, 8:00 a.m. to 5:00
p.m.
Official college office.
Career counseling, continuing
education courses.
No registration fee. Other fees vary.

CONNECTICUT

CONNECTICUT COLLEGE
Career Counseling and Placement
New London, Conn. 06320
(203) 442-5391 Ext. 218
Monday–Friday, 9:00 a.m. to 5:00
p.m.
Official college office.
Educational and career counseling,
job referral, placement.
No fees.

HARTFORD COLLEGE
Counseling Center
50 Elizabeth Street
Hartford, Conn. 06115
(203) 236-5838
Monday–Friday, 8:30 a.m. to 4:30
p.m.
College sponsored office.
Educational and career counseling,
continuing education courses, job
referral, placement.
Registration fee only.

NEW CONCEPT
111 Saugatuck Avenue
Westport, Conn. 06880
(203) 226-5841
Monday–Friday, 9:30 a.m. to 3:30
p.m.
Independent private agency.
Job referral, resume preparation,
placement.
No registration fee. Other fees vary.

UNIVERSITY OF CONNECTICUT
Continuing Education for Women,
U-56W

Storrs, Conn. 06268
(203) 486–3441
Monday–Friday, 8:30 a.m. to 4:30
p.m.
Official college office.
Educational and career counseling,
continuing education courses.
Fees vary.

YALE UNIVERSITY WOMEN'S
ORGANIZATION
Information and Counseling Service
215 Park Street
New Haven, Conn. 06520
(203) 436–8242
Monday–Wednesday, 10:00 a.m. to
2:00 p.m.
Independent non-profit agency.
Educational and career counseling,
adult education courses, job
referral.
Registration fee. Other fees vary.

YOUNG WOMEN'S CHRISTIAN
ASSOCIATION
422 Summer Street
Stamford, Conn. 06901
(203) 348–7727
Monday–Friday, 8:30 a.m. to 10:00
p.m.
Saturday, 9:00 a.m. to 2:00 p.m.
National organization.
Educational and career counseling,
adult education courses.
Registration fee.

DELAWARE

McELROY & DOBAN, INC.
2115D Concord Pike, Fairfax
Wilmington, Del. 19803
(302) 658–8647
Monday–Friday, 8:15 a.m. to 5:00
p.m.
Independent private agency.
Career counseling, job referral,
resume preparation placement.
No registration fee.

Placement fee individually
negotiated.

UNIVERSITY OF DELAWARE
Division of Continuing Education
Clayton Hall
Newark, Del. 19711
(302) 738–2214
Monday–Thursday, 8:30 a.m. to 9:00
p.m.
Friday, 8:30–5:00. Saturday,
9:00–noon.
Official college office.
Educational and career counseling,
continuing education courses.
No registration fee. Other fees vary.

DISTRICT OF COLUMBIA

DISTAFFERS RESEARCH
& COUNSELING CENTER
4625a 41st Street, N.W.
Washington, D.C. 20016
(202) 362–9494
Five day, thirty hour week.
Independent non-profit agency.
Educational and career counseling,
job referral.
No registration fee. Other fees vary.

GEORGE WASHINGTON
UNIVERSITY
Continuing Education for Women
2029 K Street, N.W.
Washington, D.C. 20006
(202) 676–7036
Monday–Friday, 9:00 a.m. to 5:00
p.m.
College sponsored.
Educational and career counseling,
continuing education courses, job
referral.
Fees vary.

JOB MARKET, INC.
1816 Jefferson Place, N.W.
Washington, D.C. 20036
(202) 785–4155

Monday–Friday, 9:00 a.m. to 5:30
p.m.
Independent private agency.
Job placement.
No registration fee.
Employer pays placement fee.

FLORIDA

COUNCIL FOR CONTINUING
EDUCATION FOR WOMEN
OF CENTRAL FLORIDA, INC.
1 West Church Street, Third Floor
Orlando, Florida 32801
(305) 423–4813
Monday–Friday, 9:00 a.m. to 12:30
p.m.
Independent non-profit agency.
Educational and career counseling,
adult education courses.
No fees.

THE GREATER MIAMI COUNCIL
FOR THE CONTINUING
EDUCATION OF WOMEN
Miami-Dade Community College
300 N.E. Second Avenue
Miami, Florida 33132
(305) 577–6840
Monday–Friday, 8:30 a.m. to 5:00
p.m.
College sponsored office.
Educational and career counseling,
limited job referral, continuing
education courses.
No registration fee. Other fees vary.

ILLINOIS

APPLIED POTENTIAL
Box 19
Highland Park, Ill. 60035
(312) 432–0620
Monday–Friday, 9:00 a.m. to 5:00
p.m.
Non-profit educational corporation.
Professional counselors.

Educational, career, and personal
counseling.
No registration fee. Other fees vary.

HARPER COLLEGE COMMUNITY
COUNSELING CENTER
Palatine, Illinois 60067
(312) 359–4200
Monday–Thursday, 8:30 a.m. to 4:30
p.m., 6:00 p.m. to 10:00 p.m.
Friday, 8:30 a.m. to 4:30 p.m.
College sponsored office.
Educational and career counseling.
No registration fee. Other fees.

MORAINE VALLEY COMMUNITY
COLLEGE
Adult Career Resources Center
10900 South 88th Avenue
Palos Hills, Ill. 60465
(312) 974–4300
Monday–Friday, 9:00 a.m. to 9:00
p.m.
Official college office.
Educational and career counseling.
No registration fee.

PHILLIPS RESEARCH
FOUNDATION
126 North Wright
Naperville, Ill. 60540
(312) 357–3180
Monday–Friday, 9:00 a.m. to 5:00
p.m.
Foundation sponsored, independent
office.
Educational and career counseling,
adult education courses.
Registration fee. Other fees vary.

SOUTHERN ILLINOIS
UNIVERSITY
General Studies Division
Office of Continuing Education
Edwardsville, Ill. 62025
(618) 692–2242
Monday–Friday, 8:00 a.m. to 5:00
p.m.
Official college office.

Educational and career counseling,
continuing education courses.
No fees.

UNIVERSITY OF ILLINOIS, URBANA-CHAMPAIGN
Student Personnel Office for Married
Students and Continuing Education
for Women
610 East John Street
Champaign, Ill. 61820
(217) 333-3137
Monday–Friday, 8:00 a.m. to 5:00
p.m.
Official college office.
Educational and career counseling.
No fees.

WOMEN'S INK
2051 Ogden Avenue
Downers Grove, Ill. 60515
(312) 969-2090
Monday–Saturday, 9:00 a.m. to 9:00
p.m.
Independent private agency.
Educational and career counseling,
job referral and placement.
No registration fee. Other fees vary.

INDIANA

INDIANA UNIVERSITY
Continuing Education for Women
Owen Hall
Bloomington, Indiana 47401
(812) 337-1684
Monday–Friday, 8:00 a.m. to 5:00
p.m.
Official college office.
Educational and career counseling,
continuing education courses.
Fees vary.

UNIVERSITY CENTER FOR WOMEN
Purdue University
2101 Coliseum Blvd. East
Fort Wayne, Indiana 46805

(219) 482-5121
Monday–Friday, 8:00 a.m. to 12:00
noon.
College sponsored office.
Educational and career counseling,
continuing education courses, job
referral.
Fees vary.

IOWA

DRAKE UNIVERSITY
Women's Programs
Center for Continuing Education
Des Moines, Iowa 50311
(515) 271-2183
Monday–Friday, 8:00 a.m. to 5:00
p.m.
Official college office.
Educational and career counseling,
continuing education courses.
No fee for individual counseling.
Fee for group sessions.

UNIVERSITY COUNSELING SERVICE
Iowa Memorial Union
University of Iowa
Iowa City, Iowa 52242
(319) 353-4484
Monday–Friday, 8:00 a.m. to 5:00
p.m.
College sponsored office.
Educational, vocational, and personal
counseling.
Fees vary for non-students.

KANSAS

UNIVERSITY OF KANSAS
Student Services
Extramural Independent Study
Center
Division of Continuing Education
Lawrence, Kansas 66044
(913) 864-4792
Monday–Friday, 8:00 a.m. to 12:00
noon, 1:00 p.m. to 5:00 p.m.

College sponsored.
Educational and career counseling, continuing education (independent study, classes).
No registration fee. Other fees vary.

MASSACHUSETTS

BOSTON PROJECT FOR CAREERS
83 Prospect Street
West Newton, Mass. 02165
(617) 969-2339
Four days, 9:00 a.m. to 4:00 p.m.
Independent non-profit agency.
Educational and career counseling, job referral, placement.
Registration fee only.

CIVIC CENTER AND CLEARING HOUSE, INC.
14 Beacon Street
Boston, Mass. 02108
(617) 227-1762
Monday–Friday, 9:30 a.m. to 4:30 p.m.
Independent non-profit agency.
Educational and career counseling, job referral.
No fee for volunteer placements.
$10.00 fee for consultation of the Career and Vocational Advisory Service.

SMITH COLLEGE
Vocational Office
Pierce Hall
Northhampton, Mass. 01060
(413) 584-2700
Monday–Friday, 8:30 a.m. to 4:30 p.m.
Official college office. Restricted to alumnae.
Educational and career counseling, job referral and placement.
No fees.

WOMEN'S EDUCATIONAL & INDUSTRIAL UNION
Career Services
264 Boylston Street
Boston, Mass. 02116
(617) 536-5651
Monday–Friday, 9:00 a.m. to 5:00 p.m.
Independent non-profit agency.
Career counseling, job referral and placement.
No registration fee. Placement fees vary.

WOMEN'S OPPORTUNITY RESEARCH CENTER
Middlesex Community College
Division of Continuing Education
Spring Road
Bedford, Mass. 01730
(617) 275-1590
Monday–Friday, 9:00 a.m. to 2:00 p.m.
College sponsored office.
Educational and career counseling, continuing education courses.
Fees vary.

MICHIGAN

MICHIGAN TECHNOLOGICAL UNIVERSITY
Center for Continuing Education for Women
Houghton, Mich. 49931
(906) 487-2270
Monday–Friday, 8:00 a.m. to 5:00 p.m.
Official college office.
Educational and career counseling, continuing education courses.
No registration fee. Other fees vary.

MONTCALM COMMUNITY COLLEGE
Area Guidance Center
Sidney, Michigan 48885
(517) 328-2111
Monday–Friday, 8:00 a.m. to 5:00 p.m.
Evenings by appointment.
College sponsored office.
Educational and career counseling.
No fees.

OAKLAND UNIVERSITY
Continuum Center
Rochester, Michigan 48063
(313) 377-3033
Monday–Friday, 8:00 a.m. to 5:00
p.m.
College sponsored.
Personal, educational and career
counseling, continuing education
courses.
Fees vary.

WESTERN MICHIGAN
UNIVERSITY
Continuing Education for Women
Kalamazoo, Mich. 49001
(616) 383-1860
Monday–Friday, 8:00 a.m. to 12
noon.
Official college office.
Educational and career counseling,
continuing education courses.
Fees vary.

MINNESOTA

MINNESOTA WOMEN'S CENTER
University of Minnesota
301 Walter Library
Minneapolis, Minnesota 55455
(612) 373-3850
Monday–Friday, 7:45 a.m. to 4:30
p.m.
Official college office.
Educational and career counseling,
continuing education courses.
No fees.

MISSOURI

UNIVERSITY OF MISSOURI, ST.
LOUIS
Extension Division—Women's
Programs
8001 Natural Bridge Road
St. Louis, Missouri 63121
(314) 453-5961
Monday–Friday, 8:00 a.m. to 5:00
p.m.

Official college office.
Educational and career counseling,
adult education courses, limited
job referral.
No registration fee. Other fees vary.

WASHINGTON UNIVERSITY
Continuing Education for Women
Box 1099
St. Louis, Missouri 63130
(314) 863-0100, ext. 4264
Monday–Friday, 8:30 a.m. to 5:00
p.m.
Official college office.
Educational and career counseling,
continuing education courses.
Fees vary.

THE WOMEN'S RESOURCE
SERVICE
University of Missouri, Kansas City
1020 East 63rd Street
Kansas City, Missouri 64110
(816) 276-1472
Tuesday–Thursday, 10:00 a.m. to
2:00 p.m.
Official college office.
Educational and career counseling,
job referral, continuing education
courses.
No fees.

NEW JERSEY

BERGEN COMMUNITY COLLEGE
Community Counseling Service
295 Main Street
Hackensack, N.J. 07601
(201) 447-1500
Monday–Friday, 9:00 a.m. to 9:00
p.m.
College sponsored office.
Educational and career counseling,
adult education courses.
No fees.

DOUGLASS COLLEGE
Women's Center
Gate House

New Brunswick, N.J. 08903
(201) 247–1766 Ext. 1603
Monday–Friday, 9:00 a.m. to 12 noon
1:00 p.m. to 4:00 p.m.
Educational and career counseling,
continuing education courses.
No fees.

EDUCATIONAL & VOCATIONAL
COUNSELING SERVICE
97 Mountainview Road
Millburn, N.J. 07041
(201) 376–5226
Saturday, 9:00 a.m. to 5:00 p.m.
Other days by appointment.
Independent private agency.
Educational and career counseling.
No registration fee. Counseling fee.

EVE
Kean College of New Jersey
Union, N.J. 07083
(201) 527–2210
Monday–Friday, 8:30 a.m. to 4:30
p.m.
College sponsored.
Educational and career counseling,
job referral.
No registration fee. Other fees vary.

JEWISH VOCATIONAL SERVICE
454 Williams Street
East Orange, N.J. 07017
(201) 674–6330
Five days, thirty-seven hours.
Independent, non-profit office.
Educational and career counseling,
job referral and placement.
Fees vary.

THE PROFESSIONAL ROSTER
83 Prospect Avenue
Princeton, N.J. 08540
(609) 921–9561
Monday–Friday, 10:00 a.m. to 12:30
p.m.
Independent, non-profit organization.
Education and career counseling, job
referral.
No fees.

NEW YORK

BARNARD COLLEGE
Placement and Career Planning
Office
606 West 120th Street
New York, N.Y. 10027
(212) 280–2033
Monday–Friday, 9:00 a.m. to 5:00
p.m.
Official college office. Restricted to
alumnae.
Career counseling, job referral,
placement.
Registration fee.

FEDERATION EMPLOYMENT
& GUIDANCE SERVICE
215 Park Avenue South
New York, N.Y. 10003
(212) 777–4900
Monday–Friday, 8:30 a.m. to 4:30
p.m.
Independent non-profit agency.
Educational and career counseling,
adult education courses, job
referral, placement.
No registration fee. Other fees vary.

HOFSTRA UNIVERSITY
Institute for Community Education
Hempstead, N.Y. 11550
(516) 560–3511
Monday–Thursday, 9:00 a.m. to 8:30
p.m.
Official college office.
Educational and career counseling,
continuing education courses.
Fees vary.

HUMAN RELATIONS
WORK-STUDY CENTER
New School for Social Research
66 West 12th Street
New York, New York 10011
(212) 675–2700, Ext. 348
Monday–Friday, 9:00 a.m. to 5:00
p.m.
Official college office.

Educational counseling, continuing
education courses.
Fees vary.

HUNTER COLLEGE
Career Counseling and Placement
Room 1601, 505 Park Avenue
New York, N.Y. 10022
(212) 360-2874
Monday–Friday, 9:00 a.m. to 5:00
p.m.
Official college office. Restricted to
alumnae.
Career counseling, job referral,
placement.
No fees.

MERCY COLLEGE
Career Counseling & Placement
Office
555 Broadway
Dobbs Ferry, N.Y. 10522
(914) 693-4500
Monday–Friday, 9:00 a.m. to 5:00
p.m.
Official college office.
Career counseling, job referral.
No fees.

NEW DIRECTIONS DIVISION
Pace University
Bedford Rd. Pleasantville, N.Y.
10570
(914) 769-3200, Ext. 211
Pace College Plaza, N.Y.C. 10038
(212) 285-3000, Ext. 3688
Monday–Friday, 9:00 a.m. to 5:00
p.m.
College sponsored offices.
Educational counseling.
No fees.

OPTIONS CAREER WORKSHOPS
FOR WOMEN
(Janice LaRouche, Founder)
333 Central Park West
New York, N.Y. 10025
(212) MO 3-0970
Monday–Saturday, 9:00 a.m. to 6:00
p.m.

Independent private agency.
Career counseling.
No registration fee. Other fees vary.

ORANGE COUNTY COMMUNITY
COLLEGE
Woman's Program
Office of Community Services
115 South Street
Middletown, N.Y. 10940
(914) 343-3311
Monday–Friday, 9:00 a.m. to 5:00
p.m.
Official college office.
Educational counseling, continuing
education courses.
Fees vary.

PROFESSIONAL SKILLS ROSTER
410 College Avenue
Ithaca, New York 14850
(607) 256-3758
Monday–Friday, 9:30 a.m. to 12:30
p.m.
Independent non-profit agency.
Job referral, limited educational and
career counseling.
No fees. Suggested donation.

SYRACUSE UNIVERSITY/
UNIVERSITY COLLEGE
Women's Center for Continuing
Education
610 East Fayette Street
Syracuse, N.Y. 13202
(315) 423-3294
Monday–Friday, 9:00 a.m. to 5:00
p.m.
College sponsored office.
Educational and career counseling,
continuing education courses.
No fees.

VASSAR COLLEGE
Office of Career Planning
Poughkeepsie, N.Y. 12601
(914) 452-7000
Monday–Friday, 8:30 a.m. to 5:00
p.m.

Official college office. Restricted to
alumnae.
Educational and career counseling,
job referral, placement.
No fees.

NORTH CAROLINA

DUKE UNIVERSITY
Center for Career Development and
Continuing Education
Durham, N.C. 27708
(919) 684–6259
Monday–Friday, 8:30 a.m. to 5:00
p.m.
Official college office.
Educational and career counseling,
continuing education courses.
No registration fee. Other fees vary.

SALEM COLLEGE
Lifespan Counseling Center for
Women
Lehman Hall, Box 10548, Salem
Station
Winston-Salem, N.C. 27108
(919) 723–7961
Monday–Friday, 8:30 a.m. to 4:30
p.m.
College sponsored office.
Educational and career counseling,
adult education courses, limited
job referral.
No registration fee. Other fees vary.

OHIO

CLEVELAND JEWISH
VOCATIONAL SERVICE
13878 Cedar Road
University Heights, Ohio 44118
(216) 321–1381
Monday–Friday, 9:00 a.m. to 5:30
p.m.
Thursday, 9:00 a.m. to 6:40 p.m.
Independent non-profit agency.
Educational and career counseling,
job referral, placement.

No registration fee. Other fees vary.

PROJECT EVE
Cuyahoga Community College
2900 Community College Avenue
Cleveland, Ohio 44115
(216) 241–5966
Monday–Friday, 9:00 a.m. to 5:00
p.m.
Community service. College
sponsored office.
Individual educational and career
counseling, no fee. Group series
and programs, fees vary.

UNIVERSITY OF AKRON
1) Office of Student Services
   Akron, Ohio 44325
   (216) 375–7425
   Monday–Friday, 8:00 a.m. to 5:00
   p.m.
2) Evening College
   Akron, Ohio 44325
   (216) 375–7791
   Monday–Thursday, 8:00 a.m. to
   9:00 p.m.
   Friday, 8:00 a.m. to 5:00 p.m.
   Saturday, 8:00 a.m. to 1:00 p.m.
Educational and career counseling,
adult education courses, job
referral, placement.
No registration fee.

OREGON

WOMEN'S PROGRAMS, DIVISION
   OF CONTINUING EDUCATION
Oregon State System of Higher
   Education
1633 S.W. Park Avenue
Box 1491
Portland, Oregon 97207
(503) 229–4849
Monday–Friday, 8:30 a.m. to 4:30
p.m.
Official college office.
Educational and career counseling,
continuing education courses.
No registration fee. Other fees vary.

PENNSYLVANIA

BRYN MAWR COLLEGE
Office of Career Planning &
  Placement
Bryn Mawr, Pa. 19010
(215) LA 5–1000, Ext. 397
Monday–Friday, 9:00 a.m. to 5:00
  p.m.
Official college office.
Educational and career counseling.
Job referral and placement.
No fees.

CEDAR CREST COLLEGE
Career Planning Office
Allentown, Pa. 18104
(215) 437–4471
Monday–Friday, 8:30 a.m. to 4:30
  p.m.
Official college office.
Educational and career counseling,
  continuing education courses, job
  referral and placement.
No fees.

INSTITUTE OF AWARENESS
401 South Broad Street
Philadelphia, Pa. 19147
(215) KI 5–4400
Monday–Friday, 9:00 a.m. to 5:00
  p.m.
Independent non-profit agency.
Educational and career counseling,
  adult education courses, special
  workshops, training programs.
Fees vary.

JOB ADVISORY SERVICE
Chatham College
Pittsburgh, Pa. 15232
(412) 441–8200, Ext. 256
Mon. Tues. Thurs. 10:00 a.m. to
  2:00 p.m.
Independent non-profit office.
Job referral.
No fees.

OPTIONS FOR WOMEN
8419 Germantown Avenue
Philadelphia, Pa. 19118
(215) CH 2–4955
Monday–Friday, 9:30 a.m. to 3:00
  p.m.
Independent non-profit agency.
Educational and career counseling,
  adult education courses, job
  placement.
No registration fee. Other fees vary.

ROBERT MORRIS COLLEGE
Department of Continuing Education
610 Fifth Avenue
Pittsburgh, Pa. 15219
(412) 471–3920
Monday–Friday, 9:00 a.m. to 5:00
  p.m.
Official college office.
Educational counseling, continuing
  education courses.
Fees vary.

SWARTHMORE COLLEGE
Office of Career Counseling &
  Placement
Swarthmore, Pa. 19081
(215) KI 4–7900
Monday–Thursday, 9:30 a.m. to 3:00
  p.m.
Official college office. Restricted to
  alumnae.
Educational and career counseling,
  job referral, placement.
No fees.

TEMPLE UNIVERSITY
Career Services/Continuing
  Education for Women
Philadelphia, Pa. 19122
Monday–Friday, 8:30 a.m. to 4:30
  p.m.
College sponsored offices.
(215) 787–7981—Career services
  Career counseling and job referral
  No counseling fee. $10.00 per year
  for employment referral.

(215) 787–7602—Continuing
Education
Educational counseling, continuing
education courses.
No registration fee.

VILLA MARIA COLLEGE
Career Counseling Center For Adult
Women
2551 West Lake Road
Erie, Pa. 16505
(814) 838–1966
Monday–Friday, 9:00 a.m. to 4:00
p.m.
Official college office.
Educational and career counseling,
job referral, placement, adult
education courses.
No fees.

TEXAS

THE UNIVERSITY OF TEXAS AT
AUSTIN
Continuing Education of Women and
Men
Office of the Dean of Students
Austin, Texas 78712
(512) 471–1201
Monday–Friday, 8:00 a.m. to 5:00
p.m.
College sponsored office.
Educational and career counseling.
No fees.

WOMEN FOR CHANGE CENTER
2001 Bryan Tower, Suite 290
Dallas, Texas 75201
(214) 741–2391
Monday–Friday, 9:30 a.m. to 3:30
p.m.
Independent non-profit agency.
Educational and career counseling,
adult education courses, job
referral.
Fees vary.

VIRGINIA

MARY BALDWIN COLLEGE
Career & Personal Counseling
Center
Staunton, Virginia 24401
(703) 885–0811, Ext. 323 or 294
Monday–Friday, 9:00 a.m. to 1:00
p.m.
2:00 p.m. to 5:00 p.m.
College affiliated office.
Educational and career counseling.
Fees vary.

UNIVERSITY OF VIRGINIA
Office of Career Planning &
Placement
5 Minor Hall
Charlottesville, Va. 22903
(703) 924–3378
Monday–Friday, 8:00 a.m. to 5:00
p.m.
Official college office.
Educational and career counseling,
limited job referral and placement.
No fees.

WASHINGTON

INDIVIDUAL DEVELOPMENT
CENTER, INC.
(I.D. CENTER)
310 15th East
Seattle, Washington 98112
(206) 329–0600
Monday–Friday, 9:00 a.m. to 4:00
p.m.
Independent private agency.
Life planning, career counseling,
adult education courses, job
referral.
No registration fee. Other fees vary.

UNIVERSITY OF WASHINGTON
Women's Guidance Center
1209 N.E. 41st
Seattle, Washington 98195
(206) 543–2100

Monday–Friday, 8:00 a.m. to 5:00
p.m.
Official college office.
Educational and career counseling,
adult education courses, limited
job referral.
Registration fee. Other fees vary.

WISCONSIN

PART-TIME PROFESSIONALS
Office of Adult Education
University of Wisconsin
Green Bay, Wisconsin 54302
(414) 465–2102
Monday–Friday, 8:00 a.m. to 5:00
p.m.
College and community sponsored.

Educational and career counseling,
adult education courses, job
referral, placement.
Fees vary.

WYOMING

UNIVERSITY OF WYOMING
Placement Service
P.O. Box 3195, University Station
Laramie, Wyoming 82071
(307) 766–2398
Monday–Friday, 8:00 a.m. to 5:00
p.m.
Official college office, restricted to
students and alumnae.
Educational and career counseling,
job referral.
No fees.

WOMEN'S UNITS IN 67 ORGANIZATIONS

Academy of Management
Committee on the Status of Women in the Management Profession.
Chair: Kathryn M. Bartol
Dept. of Mgt., School of Business Admin.
U. of Massachusetts, Amherst, Mass. 01002

Adult Education Association
Commission on the Status of Women in Adult Education
Chair: Yvonne Rappaport, Consortium Bldg.,
George Mason U., Fairfax, Va. 22030

American Academy of Religion* Task Force on the Status of Women—The Academic Study of Religion
Co-Chairs: Mary K. Wakeman, Dept. of Religious Studies Univ. of N.C., Greensboro, NC 27412; Margaret M. Early, Dept. of Religious Studies, Alverno College, Milwaukee, WI 53215.

American Anthropological Association*
Committee on the Status of Women in Anthropology
Co-Chairs: Carol Vance, Dept. of Anthropology, Columbia U., New York 10027; Lucie W. Saunders, Dept. of Anthropology, Lehman College, Bronx, N.Y. 10467

American Association for the Advancement of Science
Women's Caucus of the A.A.A.S.
Chair: Virginia Walbot, Dept. of Biochemistry, U. of Georgia, Athens, Ga. 30601

American Association for Health & Physical Education
Committee on Women
Chair: Ione G. Shadduck, Drake U., Des Moines, Iowa 50311

American Association of Immunologists*
Committee on the Status of Women
Chair: Helene C. Rauch, Dept. of Medical Microbiology, Stanford U., School of Medicine, Stanford, Cal. 94305

American Association of University Professors
Committee on the Status of Women in the Profession
Chair: Mary Gray, Dept. of Mathematics, American University, Wash., DC 20016;
Contact: Margaret Rumbarger, Associate Secretary, A.A.U.P., One Dupont Circle, Washington 20036

American Astronomical Society
Working Group on the Status of Women in Astronomy
Chair: Anne P. Cowley
Research Associate, Astronomy Dept.
U. of Michigan, Ann Arbor, Mich. 48103

American Chemical Society
Women Chemists Committee
Chair: Susan Collier, Research Lab.,
Eastman Kodak Co., Rochester, N.Y. 14650

American College Personnel Association
Women's Task Force
Chair: Mary Howard, Federal City College,
425 Second Street, NW, Washington 20001

American Economic Association
Committee on the Status of Women in the Economics
Profession
Chair: Carolyn S. Bell, Wellesley College,
Wellesley, Mass. 02181

American Educational Research Association
Women's Caucus
Chair: Noele Krenkel, Researcher, San Francisco Unified
School District, 135 Van Ness, San Francisco, Cal.
94102

American Federation of Teachers
Women's Rights Committee
Chair: Marjorie Stern, 1012—14th Street, NW,
Washington 20004

American Historical Association*
Committee on Women Historians
Chair: Jane deH. Matthews
    U. of North Carolina, Greensboro, N.C. 27412
Staff Liaison: Eleanor Straub, 400 A Street, SE,
    Washington 20003
Coordinating Committee on Women in the Historical
Profession
Chair: Sandi Cooper, Richmond College, C.U.N.Y., Staten
Island, N.Y. 10301

American Institute of Planners
Women's Rights Committee
Chair: Diana C. Donald, 1776 Mass. Ave., NW,
Washington 20036

American Library Association*
Social Responsibilities Round Table
Task Force on the Status of Women
Chair: Lynne Rhodes
    4004 Whitman North, Seattle, Wash. 98103

American Mathematical Society
Association for Women in Mathematics (Independent
group)
Chair: Mary Gray, Dept. of Mathematics,
American University, Washington 20016

American Personnel and Guidance Association
Women's Caucus
Correspondent: Beverly B. Clark, 10649 Weymouth St.,
Bethesda, Md. 20014

American Philological Association
Women's Caucus
Chair: Sarah B. Pomeroy, Hunter College, Box 1264, 695
Park Avenue, New York 10021
Committee on the Status of Women
Chair: Mary R. Lefkowitz, Dept. of Greek & Latin,
Wellesley College, Wellesley, Mass. 02181

American Philosophical Association
Women's Caucus
Chair: Mary Mothersill, Dept. of Philosophy,
Barnard College, New York 10027
Society for Women in Philosophy (Independent Group)
Chair: Hannah Hardgrave, Dept. of Philosophy,
Western Illinois U., Macomb, Ill. 61455

American Physical Society*
Committee on Women in Physics
Chair: Esther Conwell, Physics Research Lab.,
Xerox Sq. W—114, Rochester, N.Y. 14644

American Physiological Association
Task Force on Women in Physiology
Chair: Elizabeth Tidball, Dept. of Physiology,
George Wash. U. Medical Center, 2300 Eye St.,
NW, Washington 20037

American Political Science Association*
Committee on the Status of Women in the Profession
Chair: Carole Parsons, 2400 Virginia Ave., NW, #1102,
Washington 20037
Women's Caucus for Political Science
Chair: JoAnne Aviel, Calif. State, San Francisco, CA 94132
Permanent address of caucus: Mount Vernon
College, 2100 Foxhall Rd., NW, Washington 20007

American Psychological Association
Ad Hoc Committee on Women in Psychology
Chair: Martha Mednick, Dept. of Psychology,
Howard U., Washington 20001
Staff Liaison: Brenda Gurel, A.P.A. 1200 17th St.,
NW, Washington 20036

American Public Health Association
Women's Caucus
Correspondent: Mary Plaska, A.P.H.A. Women's
Caucus, 1015—16th St., N.W., Washington 20036

American Society of Biological Chemists
Subcommittee on the Status of Women
Chair: Loretta Leive, Bldg. 4, Rm. 111,
National Institutes of Health, Bethesda, Md. 20014

American Society for Microbiology*
Committee on the Status of Women Microbiologists
Chair: Mary L. Robbins, School of Medicine and
Health Sciences, George Wash. U.,
2300 Eye St., NW, Washington 20037

American Society for Public Administration
Standing Committee on Women in Public Administration
Chair: Ms. June Martin, Rm. 830,
State Leg. Bldg., Albany, NY 12224

American Society for Training and Development
Women's Caucus
Steering Committee: Shirley McCune, Center for Human
Relations, N.E.A., 1201—16th St., NW, Washington
20036; Althea Simmons, Director of Training,
N.A.A.C.P., 200 E. 27th St., New York 10016

American Sociological Association
Ad Hoc Committee on the Status of Women in Sociology
Chair: Cora B. Marrett, Dept. of Sociology,
Western Michigan U., Kalamazoo, Mich. 49001
Sociologists for Women in Society
(Independent group, formerly a caucus)
Chair: Joan Huber, Dept. of Sociology, U. of Illinois,
Urbana, Ill. 61801

American Speech and Hearing Association
Subcommittee on the State of Women
Chair: Dorothy K. Marge, 8011 Longbrook Rd., Springfield, Va. 22152

American Statistical Association
Caucus for Women in Statistics
Chair: Donna Brogan, Dept. of Statistics and Biometry, Emory U., Atlanta, Ga. 30322
Committee on Women in Statistics
Chair: Jean D. Gibbons, College of Commerce and Business Administration, U. of Alabama, University, Ala. 35486

American Studies Association
Committee on Women
National Coordinator: Joanna S. Zangrando, 501 Mineola Ave., Akron, Ohio 44320

Association of American Geographers
Committee on Women in Geography
Chair: Anne Larrimore, Dept. of Geography, U. of Michigan, Ann Arbor, Mich. 48104

Association of American Law Schools*
Committee on Women in the Legal Profession
Presiding Members: Ruth B. Ginsburg; Columbia Law School, 435 West 116th St., New York 10027; Shirley R. Bysiewicz, U. of Connecticut School of Law, 1280 Asylum Ave., West Hartford, Conn. 06105

Association of Asian Studies
Committee on the Status of Women
Chair: Joyce K. Kallgren, Center for Chinese Studies, 2168 Shattuck Ave., Berkeley, Cal. 94705

Association of Women in Architecture*
President: Dorothy G. Harrison, 2115 Pine Crest Dr., Altadena, Cal. 91001

Association for Women in Psychology*
Public Relations Editor: Leigh Marlowe, Manhattan Community College, 180 West End Ave., New York 10023
Correspondent: Dorothy Camara, 70012 Western Ave., Chevy Chase, Md. 10023
Liaison: Dolores Muhich, 516 S. University Ave., Carbondale, Ill. 62901

Association of Women in Science* **(Independent group)**
President: Estelle Ramey, 1818 R St., NW, Washington 20009

Biophysical Society*
Professional Opportunities for Women of the Biophysical Society—Caucus of Women Biophysicists
Chair: Daphne Hare, School of Medicine, S.U.N.Y. Buffalo, N.Y. 14215

Church Employed Women*
Contact: Mildred G. Lehr, The Westminster Press, 900 Witherspoon Bldg., Philadelphia 19107

College Art Association
Commission on the Status of Women in Art and Women's Caucus
Chair: Ann Harris, 560 Riverside Dr. #17P, New York 10027
President: Dolores B. Schmidt, R.D. 3, Slippery Rock, Pa. 16057

College Music Society
Women's Caucus
Co-Chairs: Carolyn Raney, Peabody Conservatory of Music, Baltimore, Md. 21202; Adrienne F. Block, Dept. of Performing & Creative Arts, Staten Island Community College, N.Y. 10301

Graduate Women in Science (Sigma Delta Epsilon)
President: Hope Hopps, 1762 Overlook Dr., Silver Spring, Md. 20903

Latin American Studies Association
Women's Coalition of Latin Americanists
Co-Chair: Elsa M. Chaney, Dept. of Pol. Sci., Fordham U., Bronx, N.Y. 10458; Asuncion Lavrin, 8501 Manchester Rd., Silver Spring, Md. 20901
Women's Committee
Chair: Nancie L. Gonzalez, Dept. of Anthropology, Boston U., Boston 02215

Linguistic Society of America
Women's Caucus
Correspondents: Lynette Hirschman, Georgette Loup, 162 W. Hansberry, Philadelphia 19144

Modern Language Association*
Commission on the Status of Women in the Profession
Chair: Dr. Elaine Reuben, 364 Bascom Hall, U. of Wisc., Madison 53706
Women's Caucus

National Association of Bank Women*
Asst. Exec. Dir.: Sharon Pierce
N.A.B.W., 111 E. Wacker Dr., Chicago 60601

National Association of Student Personnel Administrators
Task Force on Women
Chair: E. Susan Petering, Asst. Dean of Students, Framingham State College, Framingham, Mass. 01701

National Association for Women Deans, Administrators, and Counselors
Executive Director: Joan McCall,
1028 Connecticut Ave., NW, Washington 20036

National Council for the Social Studies
Committee on Social Injustice for Women
Chair: Dell Felder, U. of Houston, Houston 77004

National Council of Administrative Women in Education
President: Fern Ritter, 1815 Fort Myer Dr., N., Arlington, Va. 22209

National Council on Family Relations
Task Force on Women's Rights and Responsibilities
Chair: Rose Somerville, Sociology Dept., California State College, San Diego, Cal. 92115

National Council of Teachers of English
Women's Committee
Chair: Janet Emig, Dept. of English, Rutgers U., New Brunswick, N.J. 08903

National Education Association
Women's Caucus
Chair: Helen Bain, N.E.A., 1201—16th St., NW, Washington 20036

National Vocational Guidance Association
Commission on the Occupational Status of Women
Chair: Thelma C. Lennon, Director, Pupil Personnel Services, Dept. of Public Instruction, Raleigh, N.C. 27602

Philosophy of Education Society
Women's Caucus
Chair: Elizabeth S. Maccia,
Dept. of History and Philosophy of Education, Indiana U., Bloomington, Ind. 47401
Committee on the Status of Women (same)

Population Association of America
Women's Caucus
Chair: Nancy E. Williamson, Brown U., Providence, R.I. 02912

Professional Women's Caucus
P.O. Box 1057, Radio City Station, New York 10019
President:
Sue Caplan, Esq., 743 5th Ave., N.Y., N.Y. 10022

Society for Cell Biology
Women in Cell Biology

Chair: Virginia Walbot, Dept. of Biochemistry, U. of Georgia, Athens, Ga. 30601

Society of American Archivists
Ad Hoc Committee on the Status of Women in the Archival Profession
Chair: Mabel Deutrich, Director, Military Archives Div., National Archives & Records Service, Washington 20408

Society of Women Engineers*
Executive Secretary: Winifred D. White, 345 E. 47th St., New York 10017

United Presbyterian Church in the U.S.A.
Task Force on Women
Co-Chairs: Patricia Doyle and Elaine Homrighouse, Board of Christian Education, United Presbyterian Church, Witherspoon Bldg., Philadelphia 19107

Women Architects, Landscape Architects, and Planners
39 Martin St., Cambridge, Mass. 02138

Women in Communications*
President: Ms. Margot Sherman, One Stoneleigh Pl., Bronx, N.Y. 10708

A number of these organizations have recently formed a federation to coordinate their efforts, share resources, and promote professional career opportunities for women:
Federation of Organizations for Professional Women
1346 Conn. Ave. NW, Suite 1122
Washington, D.C. 20036

* These groups all have a known roster of women. Others have channels through which women may be referred or contacted.

Authors' Note

This booklet was prepared by Helen S. Farmer, PhD and Thomas E. Backer, PhD as part of a project sponsored by the National Institute of Education and conducted by the Human Interaction Research Institute (Los Angeles). *New Career Options for Women: A Counselors' Sourcebook* is a companion volume to this booklet, and is designed to be used by career counselors who work with women and girls.